愛護我們的地球

Sharing the Planet | Non-Fiction Series

Copyright © 2022 by Level Learning, INC. and Washington Yu Ying PCS™
Original and Edited Text Copyright © 2022 by Washington Yu Ying PCS™

All rights reserved. No part of this book in whole or part may be reproduced without written permission from the publisher.

Published by Level Learning, INC.

Content Contributors:
Washington Yu Ying PCS™ - Qianyi (Shirley) Zhang, Pearl Zao He You
Level Learning - Jingyao Qi

Illustrations by: Josh Taira

Leveling classification based on Level Learning standard. For full description, visit www.levellearning.com

ISBN 978-1-64040-070-2
Traditional Chinese Edition

About Level Learning:
Level Learning provides a literacy focused curriculum specifically designed for K-12 Chinese as a Second Language classrooms. Our program offers 20 levels of specific and detailed objectives, leveled texts and passages, mastery-based online assessment, and analytics to enable data-driven instruction. Level Learning reading curriculum for both literature and informational text emphasize grammar and comprehension skills to help teachers develop confident and independent Chinese language readers. The non-fiction series of books are specifically designed to support our informational text course based on multiple national standards. To learn more about our entire offering, visit www.levellearning.com.

About Washington Yu Ying PCS™:
Washington Yu Ying PCS is a Mandarin English dual language immersion International Baccalaureate (IB) World school. Yu Ying's mission is to inspire and prepare young people to create a better world by challenging them to reach their full potential in a nurturing Chinese/English educational environment. Yu Ying's comprehensive IB, dual immersion curriculum equips students with global competencies for success in the real world. As a leader in immersion education, Yu Ying is determined to advance Chinese language programs and global citizenry education by helping other schools create and strengthen their Chinese programs. For more information, email: products@washingtonyuying.org

人們的生活離不開空氣、水、食物和能源。可是環境污染和能源浪費卻每天都在發生著。

3

污染主要是一些有害的垃圾引起的。這些垃圾可能是人們每天的生活垃圾，可能是工業垃圾，也可能是農業垃圾等等。

如果有害的固體垃圾進入泥土中，農作物就會被污染；有害的液體垃圾流入河裡，水源就會被污染；有害的氣體垃圾飄到空中，空氣就會被污染。

這些污染都會危害人們的健康。我們要怎樣減少污染和浪費呢？

第一，我們可以多使用可回收或可分解的生活用品。這樣就會減少有害的固體垃圾。第二，我們可以節約用電。要知道，發電廠是製造液體垃圾最多的工廠之一。減少用電就會減少水源污染。

第三，我們可以少開車，多騎自行車或乘坐公共交通工具。這樣就會減少空氣污染。第四，我們可以節約用水。刷牙的時候，要記得把水關掉，把雨水存起來澆花，不要長時間洗澡等。

另外,我們也可以多種樹,把家裡的垃圾分類,減少使用塑料製品,不浪費食物等。這些事,看起來都是小事情,可是都會幫助我們減少污染,減少浪費。

地球是我們的家園。愛護地球，從每一個人做起，從每一件小事做起。

Glossary

	Pinyin	English Definition
空氣	kōng qì	air
能源	néng yuán	energy, power source
環境	huán jìng	environment
污染	wū rǎn	pollution
浪費	làng fèi	to waste
害	hài	harm
垃圾	lā jī	waste
工業	gōng yè	industry
農業	nóng yè	farming, agriculture
固體	gù tǐ	solid
農作物	nóng zuò wù	crop
液體	yè tǐ	fluid
水源	shuǐ yuán	water supply
氣體	qì tǐ	gas
飄	piāo	to float

	Pinyin	English Definition
危害	wēi hài	to harm
減少	jiǎn shǎo	to reduce
使用	shǐ yòng	to use
回收	huí shōu	recycle
分解	fēn jiě	decompose
用品	yòng pǐn	products
節約	jié yuē	to conserve
電	diàn	electricity
發電廠	fā diàn chǎng	power plant
製造	zhì zào	to make, to manufacture
工廠	gōng chǎng	factory
騎	qí	to ride
自行車	zì xíng chē	bicycle
公共	gōng gòng	public
交通工具	jiāo tōng gōng jù	transportation

Glossary

	Pinyin	English Definition
刷牙	shuā yá	to brush teeth
關掉	guān diào	to turn off
存	cún	to save
澆花	jiāo huā	to water plants
分類	fēn lèi	to sort
塑料	sù liào	plastics
地球	dì qiú	earth
家園	jiā yuán	homeland
愛護	ài hù	care

www.ingramcontent.com/pod-product-compliance
Lightning Source LLC
Chambersburg PA
CBHW041222070526
44584CB00001B/59